WITHDRAWN
WITHDRAWN

◁ **W9-AMX-395**

RHINOCEROS

THE WILDLIFE IN DANGER SERIES

Louise Martin

Rourke Enterprises, Inc.
Vero Beach, Florida 32964

LIBRARY OF CONGRESS
Library of Congress Cataloging-in-Publication Data

Martin, Louise, 1955-
  Rhinoceros   / by Louise Martin.

   p. cm. — (Wildlife in danger)
   Includes index.
   Summary: Describes the five remaining species of
rhinoceros, poaching activities which are steadily killing off
the animals, and efforts to save the rhinoceros.
   ISBN 0-86592-997-1
   1. Rhinoceros — Juvenile literature. 2. Endangered
species — Juvenile literature. 3. Wildlife conservation —
Juvenile literature. [1. Rhinoceros. 2. Rare animals
3.Wildlife conservation.] I. Title. II. Series:
Martin, Louise, 1955-
Wildlife in danger.
QL737.U63M38 1988
333.95'9 - dc19   88-10316
                 CIP
                 AC

*Title page photo: Indian
Rhinoceros (Rhinocereus
unicorns)*

TABLE OF CONTENTS

RHINOCEROSES

The rhinoceros family is about 60 million years old. Back then, many types of rhinoceros lived all over the world — in Europe, Asia, and Africa, as well as in North America. Now there are only five species left in the world: the black, the white, the Indian, the Sumatran, and the Javan. All of these rhinoceroses are in danger of **extinction**, wherever they live. No one is allowed to kill rhinoceroses for any reason.

White rhinoceroses live in Africa

WHERE THEY LIVE

The black and white rhinoceroses live in Africa. Once they were found in many parts of Africa, but today they are scarce. Too many have been killed by people. The Indian rhinoceros used to be common all over India. It is now seen only in India's mountainous region and in Nepal, a small country north of India. The Sumatran and Javan rhinoceroses are also at risk. There are only about 500 Sumatran rhinoceroses left in all of Malaysia and Indonesia. The last fifty Javan rhinoceroses live on a reserve in Indonesia.

There are only fifty Javan rhinoceroses left

WHAT THEY EAT

Rhinoceroses are **vegetarians**. They do not eat other animals, but live on a diet of coarse grass and leaves. There is always plenty for them to eat in the wild, whether they live in the African grasslands or the Indonesian jungle. Rhinoceroses are big, powerful animals. The largest, the Indian rhinoceros, stands six feet high at the shoulder. No other creatures in the wild dare to attack them. Only humans threaten the survival of the rhinoceroses.

9

A black rhinoceros feeds on swamp grasses

THREATS TO RHINOCEROSES

The problem with humans is two-fold. First of all, the human population is growing so fast that there is little room left for animals. In India and the Far East, the forests and jungles are being cleared to make room for people. The rhinoceroses are being pushed into smaller and more isolated areas, where they do not have enough room to live. An even bigger problem is that over the centuries, humans hunted the rhinoceros almost to extinction. They killed them for their horns.

Rhinoceroses need plenty of space

Rhinoceros horn is made of keratin

A black rhinoceros with its twin horns

RHINOCEROS HORNS

Some people believe that rhinoceros horns can work magic. Others use them to make medicine. Rhinoceros horns are made of **keratin**, which looks like coarse, matted hair. Scientists have proved that rhinoceros horns have no special powers, but people's beliefs are hard to change. Rhinoceros horns are also in great demand in the Middle East countries, where they are made into dagger handles.

Indian rhinoceroses have a single horn

HUNTING RHINOCEROSES

People still hunt and kill rhinoceroses even though it is now against the law. But the areas where rhinoceroses live are difficult to police. The hunters, called **poachers**, go out secretly into the jungle or the savannah and are able to kill the rhinoceroses before the police catch up with them. They hack off the horns and leave the body of the rhinoceros to rot.

These two white rhinoceroses live in the San Diego Wild Animal Park

POACHERS

Poachers earn a lot of money by selling rhinoceros horns. An African rhinoceros horn that weighs about three and a half pounds will sell for $15,000. A rhinoceros horn from one of the Asian species will sell for even more — possibly $35,000 — because it is believed that their magic is stronger. Poachers who are caught are severely punished, but so much money is at stake that they are prepared to take that risk.

Some people believe rhinoceros horns have special powers

WHITE RHINOCEROSES

There are two **sub-species** of white rhinoceros, northern and southern. A hundred years ago scientists feared the southern white rhinoceros would soon become extinct. But with careful planning, their numbers have been increased to 3,500. Now the northern white rhinoceroses are in trouble. Scientists believe there are only 17 of them left in the wild. The northern white rhinoceros is the most endangered animal in the world.

Rhinoceros horns are made into ornaments and medicines

HOW WE CAN HELP

The only way to save the rhinoceros is to stop the trade in their horns. The **World Wildlife Fund**, an organization concerned with saving rare animals, is trying to do that. It asks people who buy rhinoceros horn to think about alternatives. There is really no need to use rhinoceros horn, and it has been proved to have no medicinal value.

Glossary

extinction (ex TINK shun) - the end of a species

keratin (KER uh tin) - chemical fibers that make up animals' horns

poachers (POE churz) - people who hunt animals without permission

sub-species (SUB SPEE seez) - a scientific term meaning a group within a species

vegetarian (ve ge TAR ee an) - an animal or person that does not eat meat

World Wildlife Fund - an organization that helps save rare plants and animals

INDEX